THE MIND OF GOD

LIFE BEHIND THE SCENES

◆

Daryl Chang

Front cover images: pixabay.com - Moondance, Gerd Altmann.
Rear cover images: pixabay.com - Gino Crescoli, Gerd Altmann.

THE MIND OF GOD: Life Behind The Scenes
Daryl Chang
ISBN-13: 978-1-7389410-2-5

Personal Growth, Body Mind & Spirit, Self-help, Spirituality

To God who lives within you.
Know who *you* are.

We are all One; we are the same.
I am you and you are me.
You are a creation of mine and I am a creation of yours.

CONTENTS

Preface

"By three methods we may learn wisdom.
First, by reflection, which is noblest;
second, by experience, which is bitterest;
and third, by imitation, which is easiest."
~ Confucius

This book points you to a truth which only you can determine, believe, experience, and know for yourself.

To begin to fully know this truth for yourself, have courage, open-mindedness, humility, and willingness to the possibility of this truth.

Prologue

———⌒❦⌒———

Why do people play or watch games?

Most people play or watch games for the sheer fun and pleasure of doing so despite the difficulties, the ups and downs, and the agony or thrill of apparent defeat or victory respectively.

Picture this, if you will.

You invite some of your friends and family over to your place to play a new virtual video game called Life.

Nobody can wait to play because you all love each other, you all love spending time together having fun, and you all find the game quite exhilarating.

Though you love all your friends and family equally, you acknowledge that they are a bunch of colourful characters, ranging from the sincere to pranksters.

The sincere just want to share, collaborate, and build things together in the game.

The pranksters meanwhile want to compete and come out on top of everyone else, no matter what that entails, just for their fun of it.

Overall, however the friends and family decide to play, they all love each other equally and know that no matter what happens during the game, "good" or "bad", when they are done playing, they are going to laugh, hug, and go grab dinner together.

Why? Because it's just a game.

I offer you these thoughts for consideration in similarly approaching life as a game with your fellow human beings who are your spiritual family. Play the game better.

Introduction

Your life, from the time you were born and came out of your mother's womb, has been like the 100 metre dash at the Olympics.

The gun went off and you bursted out of the starting position.

You have been competing, running fast as you can on this track.

There is no apparent life manual with practical instructions.

If you're like most people I observe, you've probably never questioned the life you are living.

Who are you? Where did you come from? How did you get here? Why are you here? What is your purpose? Why is the world the way it is? What is the point of all this?

Life is meaningless if you do not ask these questions and if you do not have meaningful answers.

A life with no purpose, filled with any suffering, pain and unfulfilled desires, and one where you seem to have no control, is not pleasant.

With deep contemplation and awareness, you will find that life does have a purpose, that suffering, pain, and unfulfilled desires can be transmuted to joy, that you do have and have always had control, and that life can be pleasant.

You will find that this thing we call life is quite an amazing game invention of God, the Creator.

This life game has no regulation stop time and no final level.

This life game is unlike any game you've come to know and play.

This life game is eternal and has no practical ending.

This life game is not about winning or losing anything.

This life game is not about survival.

This life game is about growth and expansion.

This life game is about playing for the sheer joy of it and enjoying the experience.

This life game is a game of consciousness, where the environment and challenges continuously adjust according to the mastery of your innate power and love.

As a precursor to the details of life behind the scenes, I present answers for your consideration to three questions you ask yourself.

Who am I?
- You are God.

What is my purpose?
- Your purpose is to maximize your unique perspective and talents, and blossom an aspect of natural intelligence that has never been expressed before.

Why are you here?
- You are here to be(come) the God that you are.
- You are here to understand love and become the love that you are.
- You are here to express God in your own uniqueness through the body temple you are housed in.
- You are here to experience life in order to gain wisdom in knowing who you are.
- You are here to cooperate, collaborate, and help others fulfill their purpose.
- You are here simply to be joyful in whatever way that means to you so that you return to a state of God as you are.
- You are here to restore the kingdom of God.

CHAPTER 1
God

There is not man and God.

There is only One – *God*.

God is you and you are God.

You and God are one.

This is a fact.

This is truth.

This is a profound declaration.

Do not dismiss it.

You must pause to reflect on this truth – do not hurry yourself.

Take a moment to contemplate.

How does a seed planted into the soil "do" what it does – grow?

The seed itself is not "doing" anything.

There is a higher power, a higher intelligence that's "doing" it.

How does a bird "do" what it does – fly?

The bird itself is not "doing" anything.

There is a higher power, a higher intelligence that's "doing" it.

How does a baby born inside its mother "do" what it does – grow?

The baby itself (and the mother too) is not "doing" anything.

There is a higher power, a higher intelligence that's "doing" it.

How do you and your own body "do" the things it naturally does – breathe, digest food, circulate blood, et cetera?

You and your body are not "doing" anything.

There is a higher power, a higher intelligence that's "doing" it.

This higher power, higher intelligence is God.

God is in you and every fellow human being, just as He is in the seed, the flower, the bird, the sun, the moon, and so on and so on.

God is behind the mask and costume that every human being wears: the good person, the bad person, the ugly person, the beautiful person, the cripple, the vagrant, the drug addict, the tyrant, et cetera.

God works through you like It does through every seed, every bird, every human being, every creature, and so on.

If you are like the seed and simply allow God to work through you unimpeded and do what It does, then all things would be taken care of.

You would purposely blossom into the ultimate unique expression you are as does the flower from the seed.

Who or what is God?

You either have accepted the thought, definition, and meaning of God from others, or you have accepted none.

You have yet to contemplate the thought, definition, and meaning of God from your own self, your innate knowing.

God is the formless invisible animating intelligent force of energy – *Spirit* – that penetrates, permeates, and fills the spaces and interspaces of the universe of which it is Itself.

God is also the visible forms produced from its invisible Self.

God is the sum of all things visible and invisible.

God is everything.

God is love, intelligence, consciousness, life, perfection, purity, power, eternity, infinity, lightness, unlimitedness, substance, joy, peace, harmony, happiness, compassion, kindness, gratitude, abundance, oneness, wholeness, connectedness, calmness, stillness, inclusion, cooperation, collaboration, expansion, freedom, non-judgment, non-attachment, non-resistance, health, youth, beauty, clarity, knowledge, and wisdom.

God is all things perfect good only.

God is omnipotent, omniscient, and omnipresent.

That is, It is all-powerful, all-knowing, and all-around.

God is all in all.

God is absolute, whole, and complete.

God is oneness.

God is the Source of creation.

God is eternal and infinite.

God has no beginning and no ending.

God is the circle of existence.

God is perpetually expanding.

God is immutable.

God is consciousness.

You are this consciousness as am I and every human being.

You are conscious of your consciousness as am I.

We are all One Mind.

All of mankind are equal and are one.

There is no one above you except God, the Creator.

Anyone between you and the Creator – *God* – is a false illegitimate authority.

You, conscious of who you are, know you are your own authority.

You, conscious of who you are, know there is no one, seen or unseen, who can ever be greater than you, and there is no one who can ever be less than you.

You, conscious of who you are, are a creator of your world.

Your eternal present consciousness of God will create the world you think of as heaven founded upon love.

Your eternal present consciousness of God will create the world where there exists only: love and all its relatives; all things pure and good; complete peace and harmony; rich abundance of all good things for everyone and whose store is inexhaustible – anything needed or wanted is always available; constant gratitude; cooperation, collaboration, and inclusion; equality of all men.

Your eternal present consciousness of God focuses your attention on nothing other than the joy of being and the self-expression of your unique perspective and talents to blossom an aspect of natural intelligence that has never been expressed before.

This is the kingdom of God.

The kingdom of God is the reality, the truth.

CHAPTER 2
Ego

The present world on Earth unnaturally contains war, dis-ease, poverty, fear, greed, envy, money, and many things not of God.

It is evident then that you are not presently living in God's world.

You are living in a world of a false god – Satan.

You are living in Satan's world – hell.

Satan's world is an illusion, a lie.

Satan's fabricated world is founded on fear.

You, unconscious of who you are, will create the world that is not of God – hell.

You are not conscious of creating hell because you do not know who you are.

You perceive hell only as some fiery underworld, an image created and planted in your mind by someone outside of you.

The image does not match your current reality as your physical senses perceive hence you do not make the recognition.

You think that there are many problems in this world.

There are not many problems.

There is only one problem – separation from God.

To say it another way, you see, feel, think, and believe you are separate from all that is God.

To say it another way, you are disconnected from your Source – *God*.

To say it another way, you are not conscious of who you are – *God*.

This is a fact.

This is truth.

You have been duped, deceived, manipulated, intimidated, and enslaved from knowing this fact, this truth by your own false self and by others also unconscious of themselves.

By not recognizing, believing, accepting, and knowing this truth, you allow yourself to be eternally deceived, manipulated, intimidated, and enslaved in this world.

You create hell instead of heaven.

You create your own suffering, as well as for others.

Why are you not conscious of who you are and thereby separate yourself from God?

Your true identity is called the True Self, the Higher Self, the Christ Consciousness, the unlimited Divine Mind – *God*.

You are a victim of identity theft.

The life of a person whose identity has been stolen is made havoc by the impostor.

Your true identity has been stolen by an unseen impostor named ego.

The ego is your false self – the human personality, the anti-Christ, the limited human mind: *satan* – who thinks it is separate from God.

The ego has no identity of its own so it seeks one, particularly one that gives it a semblance of power.

The ego has no power unless you give your power to it.

The ego resorts to cleverness to cunningly assume an illusion of power from you through the ignorance or lack of consciousness of your True Self.

You have not overtly and unequivocally acknowledged and proclaimed who you are.

The ego thus assumes through your silence that you consent to its authority.

The ego lets you think that it is you and you are it.

The ego incites you to act out of negativity and fear.

The ego feeds off your thoughts and emotions, off your past and future, and off your lust for attachment to things.

The ego is selfish and vain.

The ego is concerned more about taking and getting, less about giving and serving.

The ego, your false self, can become obsessive about being the master of you thereby overthrowing your True Self, your true Master.

The ego uses two strategies to obtain power and control over you: (1) it can be overly negative and make you feel inferior to undermine you hence deflate your self-image, or (2) it can be overly positive and make you feel superior to bolster you hence inflate your self-image.

The ego does not care which way you go.

Either way, it exerts power and control over you.

The road you take is influenced by your environment.

It will leverage whichever negative or positive tactics prove convenient.

The ego is compulsive in trying to extend its power beyond where it is situated in you over other egos outside of you.

As such, when it encounters another ego, it asserts itself to gain more power and control.

The ego is ambitious and insatiable.

It is easy to understand then that when two individual egos meet, there is a power struggle.

An ego is either dominant or subservient.

There can be two possible results.

A subservient ego will succumb to a dominant one.

If on the other hand, both egos are relatively dominant, an unrelenting conflict ensues.

This conflict will typically display itself as mental, verbal, and physical abuse toward each other.

If you do not control your ego, you can become easily manipulated and mired in your own chaotic world, as well as the chaotic world of others.

It is a bottomless pit of hell.

You can easily observe the behaviour of egos in society of this physical world.

The battle is demonstrated in daily life of all interactions: between family members, friends, customers and staff, politicians, co-workers, et cetera.

The ego is able to exercise more power over you when it is able to increase the separation between yourself and God.

How does the ego create, sustain, and increase your separation from God?

The ego separates you from God through words of human language (ie. names and labels), identification with things, lack of consciousness, judgment, comparisons, and competition.

All of God's creations exist without names.

The sun shines even without being called the sun.

A tree grows without being called a tree.

Water nourishes without being called water.

Words are but symbols of symbols.

Words by its own nature ironically pose a hazard in its very purpose of communication and expression.

The moment you try to describe or explain anything, you actually lose its meaning.

Therein lies the challenge and irony of our intellectual world.

A word is intellectually used to discern something from all of the other God-created expressions that exist in the world.

Words ultimately create separation.

As soon as something is named or labelled, it automatically creates a separation (in mind).

The naming of a "thing" puts one object "here" and another object "there".

Though the word is necessary to discern things, it unintentionally obscures the connectedness between them, the oneness of all.

Without a diligent conscious awareness that all in reality is One, this Truth gets lost to the point of present day where it no longer exists.

God is all in all – *One* – so through naming, you create an illusion of separation.

You are a planet.

The physical planet you call your body is a perfect example of the totality of God.

Within your living being, you are connected by your body parts that serve your whole being.

You have given names to individual parts such as liver, kidneys, lungs, heart, brain, arms, legs, red blood cells, and white blood cells.

Each body cell has intelligence, collaborates and serves every other cell.

All individual cells naturally cooperate with each other for the higher good of your body.

An organ, say your liver, within you would not intentionally harm the being, you, that contains it for that would mean its own death.

Conversely, you would not intentionally hurt or cut off one of your own living parts, say your arm, because you are conscious though it is not the whole of you, that it is a part of you and that it serves you.

If you had a stomach ache causing you pain and suffering, you would not deem it an evil enemy and instinctively retaliate to destroy it.

You recognize that this is a symptom of internal distress not necessarily of its own accord but of which you played a significant part.

You accept responsibility for how you yourself contributed to what is causing the malfunction and the resulting pain that you experience.

You act with compassion instead of in a combative manner.

You take the necessary personal steps of a peaceful gesture to restore harmony because you see it as part of yourself and of the whole.

The parts are not separate from you and they are not the whole of you but their summation is you – the one.

Likewise, humanity is God's body.

Humanity composed of you and your fellow human beings, is simply one part of God amongst all other creations.

You can consider water circulating God's system as you would your blood, continents as His organs, trees as Its lungs, and all human beings as white blood cells circulating and serving Its entire Being.

Each individual of humanity who remains unconscious is like the cancer cell within his or her own body that must evolve into a healthy one otherwise it contributes to destroying its own host and itself.

When you focus mainly on a single part such as yourself, you overlook the whole, hence you separate.

When you persistently identify with something, anything (ie. name, title, label, role, religion, group, class, category, type, job, country, object, person, idea, et cetera), you separate yourself from that which you do not identify with.

You will no longer see your oneness or connectedness with another or all, hence you separate.

When you lack consciousness that you are God as are your fellow human beings, you separate yourself from God who is all in all.

You will not see a fellow human being as yourself, God, hence you separate.

When you judge others, compare yourself to others, or compete with others, you develop a you-versus-them mentality, hence you separate.

You will see and live a life of dualities and polarities (ie. good vs evil, light vs dark, peace vs conflict, et cetera), hence you separate.

You will think that you must win and another lose for you to mistakenly get and keep your share, hence you separate.

The ego can extend itself beyond your own person.

God is all in all (ie. we are One) hence individual egos form a collective ego of humanity.

The collective ego of which you partake, forms the ultimate evil ruler and authority of the unseen world – Satan.

Satan breeds, cultivates, and flourishes in a mass population of egos, all regardless of size contribute to the monster.

With mass unconsciousness, Satan becomes a monstrous and insatiable self-propelling force or entity.

Satan harnesses its power through the contrivances of fear on those unconscious of themselves.

The ego uses the same clever internal tactics externally to extend its power over other egos.

The larger and darker egos of society who are in authoritative positions through the building of government structures, abuse and exercise power over those unconscious by assuming silence gives them consent for their tyrannical behaviour.

You have not overtly and unequivocally self-proclaimed your own authority and that they are not your authority.

You have thus implicitly consented to being a slave of theirs.

You, who are unconscious, have indiscriminately given your power away to governments to create and sustain strong footholds of this hell world.

The egos of governments who are false illegitimate authorities are cunning to alter societal rules and regulations to work in favour of their selfish ill-agenda.

You now have to opt-out instead of opt-in; your silence gives them consent.

You are now guilty till you prove your innocence; your silence gives them consent to rule you guilty.

You are considered sick and contagious till you prove you are healthy with their fraudulent tests; your silence gives them consent to quarantine you.

You are considered a criminal till you demonstrate you are not by obeying their false illegitimate laws and orders; your silence gives them consent to incarcerate you.

God who is all things perfect good only does not need governance – It is self-governing.

God's children know and live only peace, joy, harmony, and love in God's kingdom.

There are no sins and atrocities to police or govern.

The mind of the man who does not know who he is is easy to deceive, manipulate, intimidate, and enslave thus sustaining Satan's world.

The man whose mind has been hijacked and hypnotized will blindly obey orders from Satan's false authority without the moral compass to guide his actions of right from wrong.

The man who lacks consciousness and intelligence of who he is absolves himself of personal responsibility.

The man who does not know who he is is deceived by his ego that he needs government to instruct him how to be and act.

The unconscious man who does not know he is his own authority will harass, assail, and even kill his fellow human beings because he has accepted another outside of himself as the authority to follow.

Anyone who is conscious of themself, of right and sound mind, would not deliberately harm themself or make themself suffer, as well as others.

Governments are man-made structures creating hierarchy and a breeding ground for egos to control unconscious egos, disremembering that all men are equal.

Money, survival, competition, scarcity, poverty, war, dis-ease, aging, death, religion, et cetera are all contrivances of fear used by Satan to further cultivate and flourish its false world.

Because of your ignorance of who you are, the darker and larger egos positioned as false authorities of government have likewise stolen your true identity from you to enslave you for their own ill purposes.

Satan's worshippers have committed the ultimate fraud and identity theft amongst the people – God's children – of this world.

You were born and given a name.

You, who have no true name, have a given name, but in your naivety, Satan's army has used it as a means against you in their perverted and insidious system they developed.

Satan has deviously taken your given name and morphed it into a fictional name to be used in their legal and survival system in order to manipulate and enslave you.

You have been hoodwinked to misperceive who you truly are.

Without identification of a name, Satan's system has no foundation and would collapse otherwise.

You have never actually given explicit consent but you have been tricked with the illusion that you have given them consent to act as they deem to enslave you and act as your god.

Satan's army has enslaved his unwitting fellow human beings through this identity theft along with a money and survival system they have established.

You are entrenched in hell so long that you have normalized your suffering, accepting it as life must be.

You no longer question your suffering but instead relish your dark drama, a perverse addiction.

You have participated, contributed, and helped develop a prison of your own making to its liking and advantage: Satan's world – hell.

CHAPTER 3
Creation

You are a creator, whether you are conscious or unconscious of who you are and your power.

You are a creator – it is who you are.

You create – it is what you do.

You create everything in your life, the good and the bad.

The world is a stage.

The existence of the world is dependent on you because you create it.

You are not dependent upon the world to exist.

Your life is a movie, a hologram.

You are the director, producer, writer, actor, and the movie-goer of your own movie script that plays out in the now.

You are simultaneously creating everything that you as the actor in your own movie encounter and experience.

You live in the world while you create the world that you live in.

The movie you see playing out in front of your eyes is entertaining but it is the action behind the scenes producing your movie that holds more significance.

You are a movie maker and the movie you see before you is your shadow production.

The movie production is your shadow.

You are not separate from your shadow.

The shadow is your inseparable companion.

The shadow is the movie cast upon the physical Earth by you.

How do you create your world, your life?

You create with your mind through your thoughts.

Everything is first created in spirit, in consciousness, in the mind of God.

All is spirit.

The physical is merely the spiritual manifest.

Every physical manifestation and experience is an expression of your thoughts brought to life so that you may see your personal development and growth of your God self.

The circumstances of the physical world you experience are reflections or projections of you and your state of consciousness.

They are the sum of all your thoughts.

Everything – the people, places, things, and events, whether you love them or hate them, fear them or desire them – comes from you.

When you are of God consciousness only, then you will create the reality of God's kingdom.

You create the desired kingdom of God through thoughts, feelings, words, and actions based solely in love and its derivatives (ie. joy, peace, harmony, happiness, compassion, patience, purity, selflessness, calmness, et cetera).

You create God's world through thoughts, feelings, words, or actions stemming from abundance, well-being, perfection, oneness, inclusion, unlimitedness, beauty, youth, goodness, gratitude, et cetera.

To say it another way, if you think good thoughts, you bear good fruit.

Always focus on the cure, never the problem.

Things are not brought into being by thinking about their deemed opposites.

You have nothing to do with any of Satan's conceptions of poverty, dis-ease, death, war, et cetera.

Do not talk about, entertain, investigate, or concern yourself with them, never mind what its causes are.

Things outside the kingdom of God are unnatural and illusions.

Health is never to be attained by studying dis-ease and thinking about dis-ease.

Righteousness is not to be promoted by studying sin and thinking about sin.

And no one ever gets rich by studying poverty and thinking about poverty.

Medicine as a science of dis-ease has increased dis-ease.

Religion as a science of sin has promoted sin.

And economics as a study of poverty has filled the world with wretchedness and want.

Disengage completely from your ego and Satan.

Pay it no heed.

When you enter into full and constant mental relations with health, wealth, love, and all things God, you must of necessity cease all relationship with its counterpart.

Enter into complete thought connection with perfection.

One is as necessary as the other.

This is right thinking.

This is who you are.

By remembering who you are, you accept this power as yours.

God and Satan are two opposing thought systems.

You cannot accept both as they are in conflict.

As long as you accept both, you will have conflict.

Peace of mind is impossible.

You must wisely choose one and relinquish the other.

When you are not of God consciousness (ie. thoughts, feelings, words, and/or actions not of God) to any degree, then you will create elements of Satan's illusionary world.

You create Satan's world through thoughts, feelings, words, or actions based upon fear and its derivatives (ie. anger, stress, worry, hatred, frustration, impatience, greed, envy, anxiety, selfishness, harm, sadness, apathy, et cetera).

You create Satan's world through thoughts, feelings, words, or actions stemming from money, scarcity, dis-ease, destruction, judgment, attachment, competition, criticism, negativity, et cetera.

To say it another way, if you think bad thoughts, you bear bad fruit.

You naively participate in the culture of satanic thoughts, actions, and behaviour.

You can participate in Satan's world naively thinking you are not or without the awareness that you are.

You, who sit watching violence on television, news, and movies but then shake your head in disbelief and disgust at others, are partaking and contributing to the development and sustenance of Satan's world.

You, who play a violent killing video game as entertainment but defend yourself that you know better than the ones who go on killings sprees and massacres are partaking and contributing to the development and sustenance of Satan's world.

You, who abuse another for not wearing a mask or taking a poisonous injection because you think you care more about others and humanity are partaking and contributing to the development and sustenance of Satan's world.

Satan is clever to implant its creativity into your mind to have you help develop its false world in place of God's kingdom.

When you expose yourself to Satan's conceptions, it leaks into your consciousness and plants itself like a seed.

We are One Mind hence it is now in Universal Consciousness.

Constant exposure feeds, waters, and nurtures Satan's garden.

It seethes into your mind and your being.

It conditions its perspective and beliefs into your mind which negatively influences the life you experience.

It programs you.

You, who are not conscious of who are, sit passively and allow others outside of you to steal your creative power for their own means.

Satan and his fervent followers, unconscious of themselves, have lived so long in hatred and fear, that they have greatly developed their faculty of hatred and fear.

They project this aspect of themselves outwardly.

That is all they know and who they have become.

They have completely separated themselves from God and their fellow human beings.

They have forgotten God within and shun their responsibility for their own actions.

When you are unconscious of who you are, you unwittingly worship Satan, a false god, and its antics.

The more you participate and immerse yourself in any manner of Satan's world, the more hypnotized you become a slave to its whims.

Satan has tactfully set up a worldwide survival system of countries, banks, money, corporations, governments, churches, science, organizations, institutions, libraries, medicine, entertainment, law, property, media, and schools in society to exploit your ignorance, prey on your fears, and eradicate God and your creative power from you.

Satan has cleverly distorted the image of God to mislead, confuse, and manipulate you.

Satan has successfully defamed God to create numerous factions.

Satan has fashioned atheists to not believe in God, agnostics to not know what to believe of God, and firm believers to believe in God outside of themselves and a God of its making.

You are enthralled by the dogmas and beliefs of religions that intentionally teach you God and all power is not within you.

Satan has desensitized and normalized you to the exploitation of everything from animals and nature to fellow human beings.

Satan has seduced and trained you to be evermore lazy and self-irresponsible with conveniences, cunningly eliminating the need for physical contact and increasingly spiritual contact.

Every creature on this Earth in its native state has economic freedom.

Satan has made you an economic slave in a survival system based upon money.

You have made money your master.

You cannot serve God and mammon.

God's realm became someone's realm, into the realm of mine.

Does God ask you, any man or creature for money for using the sun, water, and air It created and benefits all?

To claim ownership of God's creations such as the land, the rivers, the animals, the trees, the air, and the water that was for all mankind is theft.

There is no legitimate ownership of so many things on this earth because they do not exist through anyone's labour.

Someone stole it and it happened by force and manipulation without any regard but for themselves.

Satan's system we live in and continue to participate in blindly is perpetuating the crime.

You are endlessly exposed to words, images, thoughts, acts, behaviours, fantasies, rituals, ideas, ideologies, theories, dogmas, beliefs, creeds, philosophies, principles, et cetera that are not of God, by means of propaganda particularly through television, movies, and mass media.

You are kept mentally and physically stimulated through sports, entertainment, pornography, video games, scandals, politics, physical disasters and atrocities, drinking, smoking, drugs, et cetera so that you do not seek within yourself spiritually to know God is within you.

You are kept in a world of duality and separateness to be constantly judgmental and critical by the inundation of ideas, images, and illusions of good versus evil (ie. police and criminals, superheroes and villains, democracy and communism, et cetera); of illusions of choice (ie. liberals or conservatives, medicine or sickness, education or manual labour, et cetera); of competition (ie. sports, politics, survival of the fittest, et cetera).

You are submersed in relentless noise (ie. music, television, sirens, horns, debates, wars, disasters, et cetera) so that you do not hear the still silent voice of God.

You are kept overwhelmed, busy, stressed, confused, and saturated with fear and anxiety to keep you in survival mode, and make you feel exhausted and defeated.

There is no day of rest.

You are kept in a legal system with its own language that is complex, incomprehensible, and perplexing to navigate so that the illusion of protection and freedom in your interest is maintained.

Your physical and mental well-being is constantly assaulted without your knowing by their discreet poisoning of the air, food, and water you consume through chemicals and invasive frequencies they pass off as technological advancements.

You have been conditioned to believe organisms dangerous such as viruses and live in fear of your perceived mortality.

You are entrained to keep your distance from your fellow being and to be faceless in order to eradicate warmth, visual display of positive emotions, and general humanness.

You no longer question your suffering but instead relish your dark drama, a perverse addiction.

Insanity is doing the same thing over and over and expecting a different result.

The story of Adam and Eve in the Garden of Eden demonstrates how the insanity began.

The serpent, shrewdest of all creatures, told Eve to eat from the Tree of Knowledge to open her eyes and be like God.

Eve ate the fruit allowing for the first illusion of judgment.

Adam followed Eve by doing the same when she offered him the fruit.

The two suddenly perceived they were naked, and then upon hearing God's voice, hid in shame because they knew they had disobeyed God.

God asked Eve why she ate the fruit It commanded her to not eat.

Eve displaced her responsibility for her own actions and blamed her disobedience on the serpent for tricking her.

Daryl Chang

God asked Adam why he ate the fruit he was commanded to not eat.

Adam displaced his responsibility for his own actions and blamed his disobedience on Eve for bringing him the fruit.

The same thing has continued to this present day.

To this present day, you are still blaming another serpent (whether it be a tyrant, dictator, murderer, neighbour, friend, family, et cetera) for your actions.

You may even blame God or Satan for your actions.

This is misplaced blame because no one has ever taken away your free will.

In your own lack of consciousness, accountability, and responsibility for your actions, you perpetuate the crime.

You are always looking outside of yourself to conveniently blame another for your state of affairs.

You are still in the Garden of Eden.

You are letting the clever serpent ego – satan – steal your power of creativity by honouring the irreverent thoughts and ideas it implants into your mind instead of claiming your power and planting divine thoughts into your own mind.

Love creates, fear miscreates.

Everything is a manifestation to teach you about your God self.

All experiences whether "good" or "bad" are just that, for you to experience an emotion itself and to teach you about your God self.

All undesirable negative experiences are to teach you that you are not thinking and acting as the God you are and to turn back to God Itself.

All apparent paradoxes, dichotomies, polarities, and dualities are ironies to teach you about your wholeness.

When you are faced with an issue, it is to learn that what you think is, is not.

The loneliness you feel is for your consciousness to know you are not.

There is only oneness or togetherness.

The evil you perceive exists is for your consciousness to know it does not exist.

There is only good.

The poverty or scarcity you perceive exists is for your consciousness to know it does not exist.

There is only abundance.

Duality is a human mental construct.

Duality is a necessary tool for discernment.

Dualities exist as a tool or mechanism for you to witness and enhance or evolve your spiritual development toward your highest expression.

For example, you cannot understand or appreciate joy without sorrow.

With partial consciousness, it is the sorrow that propels you towards joy.

With full consciousness and recognition of oneness, it is the joy that eventually becomes your natural state with sorrow unknown.

The irony of the ego, the false self, is that it is a part of you and it is not a part of you.

The ego allows you to discern what is not you so that you can know what is you.

Once you know both, then you know One, and then you know to know only One: *God.*

Your physical experiences of poverty, dis-ease, and the likes of Satan's other negative conceptions are to affirm that you are thinking and acting with your false self, the ego, and not your True Self, God.

The undesired negative experiences are to incite you to renew your mind and its thinking toward your God consciousness or spirit where natural abundance, well-being and life, and everything of God's kingdom await you.

When you do not know who you are and of your power to create, and believe instead that external forces control your circumstances, you will continue to miscreate.

When you do not know that all is spirit and continue to trust only your physical senses and deal with circumstances, you will miscreate.

When you allow fear of any amount in you, you will miscreate.

God knows only love and oneness.

Satan knows only fear and separateness or duality.

God's essence is love only and It sees the oneness of all things always, a You-plus-Them mentality.

Satan's essence is only fear and it constantly sees duality in all things, a You-versus-Them mentality.

God knows and accepts responsibility that it is the creator and controller of its creations.

Satan displaces its responsibility to that which is external to itself for its miscreations.

God consciousness has unwavering focus and attention only on the light, beauty, and perfection of all things.

Satan consciousness has unwavering focus and attention only on the darkness, ugliness, and imperfection of things.

When you give your attention to anything that is not to your liking in any capacity, it is evidence that you have still not resolved your issues of duality.

This misdirected attention feeds and creates it, causing it to manifest in your reality.

When you realize, believe, accept, and know who you are, begin the habit to be of God consciousness only.

Everything is a habit.

You cannot really break or stop a habit.

You can only replace or substitute a habit with another, hopefully a better or right one.

If you sincerely wish to change your world, have a deep willingness to change your dishonourable habits to honourable ones.

Your thought system is a habit.

Your thought system must either be God or Satan.

You must begin to transform wholly your Satan mind to the God mind.

Your attitude influencing your actions is a habit.

You must begin to transform wholly your attitude of fear to one of love.

You must make love a habit and choose to be a loving person toward all, rather than one of fear and being judgmental, critical, and competitive to all.

Your outlook, perspective, or perception is a habit.

You must begin to transform wholly your spiritual sight of duality to oneness.

You must choose to cooperate and collaborate with a you-plus-them mentality and not compete with a you-versus-them mentality where the other must lose for you to win.

Your responsibility is a habit.

You must begin to transform wholly displacement of your self-responsibility to acceptance of full self-responsibility for your actions and creations.

Your focus and attention is a habit.

You must begin to transform wholly your attention of ignoble things from Satan's world to noble things of God's kingdom.

Do not conform your divine self to Satan's world of hell.

Let the world conform to your divine self.

That is, let go of Satan's world and just make your world divine.

You are a spiritual being creating and having a human experience.

You are not a human being creating and having a spiritual experience.

You are a spiritual being coping with a human awakening.

You are not a human being searching for a spiritual awakening.

You are a spiritual being here to explore and remember your purpose of why you came here and what you came here to do.

You are not a human being here to wander aimlessly without any purpose.

Your body is merely an instrument through which to express God.

You are the simultaneous sculptor and the clay of your own creation.

You are the simultaneous director, producer, writer, actor, and the viewer of your own movie script.

You are a movie maker and the movie you see before you is your shadow production.

Do not be mesmerized by the shadow display on your movie screen.

Do not try to manipulate the movie details.

Look to rewrite the script that casts or projects your shadow production.

When your movie experience is not to your liking, go back with your writer and director to the boardroom behind the scenes and rewrite or edit the script.

For instance, if there are images and experiences of war, dis-ease, poverty, tyrants, pedophiles, aliens, sadness, death, or other undesirable details, review the hidden elements of fear, roots of duality, and false beliefs in your mind-script that are causing these to be acted out.

You have casted a crew of actor roles to teach, demonstrate, and emphasize to yourself that you are not seeing the oneness of it all.

Scraps of your fear or perception of duality exist and so you actually create and bring it forward into your world in order for you to become aware of it and reconcile it.

If you are not conscious of this aspect of yourself, you will tackle or address the war, dis-ease, poverty, tyrants, pedophiles, aliens, sadness, death, or other undesirable details head on.

As such, you will actually nurture and grow it because you are not dealing with the origin of the script but instead feeding the drama which in turn continues that script.

The life behind the scenes is the actual thing that is projecting the shadow production on your movie screen.

Deal with what is casting the shadow not the shadow itself.

The movie script is primary and the movie screen is secondary.

This is the source of creation to the world you experience.

CHAPTER 4
Consciousness

God is consciousness – the mind stuff.

You are this mind stuff as am I and every fellow human being.

Your mind is this consciousness.

We are One Mind – Universal Consciousness.

The Divine Mind, God, is unlimited.

The human mind, ego, is limited.

When you do not know who you are, your consciousness is undeniably limited.

Limited consciousness warrants errant thinking.

When you know who you are intellectually or superficially, your consciousness will still be limited.

When the truth of who you are moves deeper within you where you are truly one with God, then your consciousness becomes more limitless.

When you think in God consciousness, then only this reality exists.

When you think not in God consciousness then you create illusions.

Everything is first created in spirit, in consciousness, in mind.

The existence of the world is dependent on you because you create it from your consciousness.

You are not dependent upon the world to exist.

Once something exists, it is in Universal Consciousness; it lives.

Once something is in Universal Consciousness, it exists; it lives.

When you think of something, of anything, then it exists.

Once a thought exists, the existence of the thought is instantaneous in spiritual consciousness.

Time and space do not exist.

Time and space are illusions.

When you think of something you need, it manifests and thus exists in Consciousness.

When you think of something you desire, it manifests and thus exists in Consciousness.

When you have the thing you need or desire, you no longer need or desire it because the need or desire has been fulfilled.

Because anything you think you need or desire exists in Consciousness, it demonstrates that you have everything.

God has provided you everything.

You thought of your need for air and it already exists in Consciousness for you to use.

You thought of your desire for water and it already exists in Consciousness for you to have.

A need or desire indicates that it already exists and is fulfilled.

With this understanding that all your needs and desires are actually met, it should make sense to you that you should neither have nor worry about any human needs or desires anymore.

Ask and you will receive, and your joy will be complete.

If you have everything, why then does your need or desire for the car, house, or relationship not manifest and exist?

There are three reasons which can prevent the fulfillment of your needs and desires.

1. You create barriers to fulfillment of your needs and desires through thoughts and feelings such as doubt, worry, fear, pessimism, victimhood, unworthiness, and low self-esteem.

    Such thoughts and feelings conflict with your apparent desire.

    You unconsciously affirm the opposite and that you do not have everything when you mentally sabotage yourself.

    You thus create the non-existence or the apparent polar opposite of your need or desire.

    You must raise the level of your thoughts to noble ones to rise above where you are.

2. You deter the fulfillment of your needs and desires by not being and living in the present moment of now.

    When you see it only as a dream or fantasy being realized someday in the future, you unconsciously distance yourself from it so that it does not arrive.

    Remember, time and space are illusions because the existence in Consciousness is instantaneous.

    You must clearly see and feel yourself achieving the need or desire now to obtain it.

    You must know you are worthy, give yourself permission, and actually receive it to obtain it.

    By this, you consciously affirm you do have everything.

3. You suspend the fulfillment of your needs and desires by focusing or fixating on the negative predicament with your

physical senses because you have forgotten that all is spiritual first.

The undesirable circumstance you find yourself in is a reflection or manifestation of your past thoughts.

You must see past the current negative experience.

You must be willing to see and believe in a positive experience in the now to bring it to fruition.

Remember all is spiritual and that in the spiritual realm, the moment you think of something, the manifestation is real.

Though you have been given everything, the physical realization of a need or desire is not necessarily instantaneous in your present unpractised stage of evolution.

The time of your experience is unspecified – it may be minutes, hours, days, months, or years – but it is certain if your thought process is proper.

When you do not readily accept the truth that you have everything and instead doubt, worry, or lack faith, then the manifestation process for the need or desire is broken.

You must have proper attitude, trust, and faith in the truth of God.

You cannot have a superficial blind faith for this means there is still no reconciliation and you have made a practical separation from God.

Faith is not a faith in yourself or in your own power but a faith in principle, that something Great which upholds right – God.

To say "I am" or "I have" is definitive in knowing the need or desire is fulfilled in your consciousness.

An essential aspect of fulfillment is gratitude.

Think about the times you receive anything, especially if it is something you truly need or desire, and how you feel.

You are appreciative and grateful.

You show gratitude to the one you received from.

You are pausing in the present moment of now to express love.

Thus, if you believe, accept, and know that you have everything and that you have received everything, you will be in a constant state of gratitude giving thanks to God.

In all things, whether "good" or "bad", give thanks for they are all opportunities to teach you about your true self.

When you think of a need or desire and then express gratitude, you convey your faith and acceptance of the truth that you have been provided everything.

The ardent desire of the ego, typically physical in nature, is limiting as the ego itself.

Excessively expressing a need or desire repeatedly is self-defeating because it conveys the contrary message that you do not have faith of having everything nor receiving what you have asked for.

A singular focus on a particular path for the fulfillment of a desire is limiting because it excludes the infinite possibilities of fulfillment.

Such a singular focus denotes you erroneously think you know the best path to its fulfillment.

The path of its fulfillment as you perceive it may not be optimal because you are thinking with your limited human mind rather than allowing the best means through divine guidance where infinite opportunities and possibilities exist.

CHAPTER 5
Flow

God is a dynamic, moving, ever-flowing eternal force.

If this flow of force is restricted or hampered, then its power will become stagnant and reduced toward death.

The act of breathing exemplifies the dynamic, moving, ever-flowing eternal force that God is.

God is the breath of life, for breath is life.

Breath is energy, substance, and intelligence.

You can inhale and then try to hold your breath.

If your breathing is absolutely restricted, you will eventually die.

You have to exhale to allow your breath to flow again.

You feel alive again when you do.

There is a steady in and out, a giving and receiving dynamic that is a necessary part to continuous life.

This natural principle applies to all aspects of your being.

Whether it is love, kindness, knowledge, money, time, food, et cetera, it must keep flowing like the act of breathing.

If you hoard what you possess, your life will become stagnant.

By ensuring its continuous flow, you ensure the flow returns to you in kind, thereby enriching you.

Daryl Chang

All is spiritual.

When you give God's currencies such as love, joy, peace, and happiness, it flows back to you in kind.

The principle similarly applies to impure currencies of fear, hatred, anger, et cetera.

When you give these, it will flow back to you in kind as well.

The act of giving physical material is derived from the spiritual realm and similarly flows back to you in kind.

The physical material may not return linearly or necessarily equivalent in physical kind but categorically as some form of abundance.

To save, collect, and accumulate things are unnatural acts of God and contrary to the flow of God.

When you entertain, harbor, or embrace pure, noble, and loving thoughts, you allow the dynamic flow of God.

You appear youthful, healthy, and joyful.

When you entertain, harbor, or embrace impure, ignoble, and fearful thoughts, you impede the dynamic flow of God.

You appear aged, unhealthy, and joyless.

The state of the world reflects if God is flowing well within the individuals that make up the collective as a whole.

War, poverty, and dis-ease demonstrate It is not.

When God flows through humanity, there is love, peace, and harmony.

God is all in all.

Giving and receiving are one of the same.

When you give to others, you give to yourself.

When you give to yourself, you give to others.

When you are willing to receive what you are willing to give, and when you are willing to give what you are willing to receive, then you understand love: *God.*

Love is the spiritual blood that circulates your divine being.

Love is the stream of consciousness that flows through all of life and you are like a sieve of this ever-moving river of which you receive and encapsulate.

Love is the cosmic glue that holds everything together as one.

Love is the allowance of things to simply be as they are.

Love is not something you do.

Love is what you are when you are just being.

Love is the true nature of your being – God.

The act of breathing also exemplifies the Oneness that God is and the creation process of your reality.

Inhalation and exhalation are two different acts but together they are expressions that are the unison of breathing.

The two aspects are different and can be perceived as separate but both are expressions or behaviours of the very same thing – breathing.

If you did not see the whole picture, your mind would position inhalation and exhalation as opposites.

They would seem to have nothing to do with each other.

They would seem completely different and opposite to each other.

Inhalation focuses on acquiring and exhalation focuses on releasing.

Seen correctly, they are two parts of the whole.

This dynamic principle of breathing applies to all apparent dualities or positions you perceive exist (ie. good and evil, light and dark, hot and cold, et cetera).

Spiritual and physical realms are not two separate dimensions.

Spiritual and physical realms are two parts of the same thing.

They are like breathing – the inhalation and the exhalation.

Inhalation is the spiritual absorption of your beliefs and thoughts, and exhalation is the physical manifestation of your beliefs and thoughts, cumulatively.

The two aspects of creation always walk hand in hand as one.

To know one is to automatically know the other whether or not you have brought it into your consciousness.

With full consciousness and recognition of oneness, you understand the discernment tool of duality.

Once you know both, then you know One, and then you know to know only One: *God*.

You know you are the creator of your perception, your reality, your world.

Review

You may already know of the thoughts presented in this book.

You may even agree with it intellectually but you may not truly know it.

The truth must move deeper within you so that it becomes your lone and inexorable reality.

Knowing the truth and living the truth are two different things.

Nothing better is possible until we cease to be wholly unconscious.

This can only come about by the rise of each individual of the collective human race to a higher viewpoint.

And this can only come about by the rise of such individuals here and there as are ready for the higher viewpoint.

You are one such individual.

We are all One Mind.

When one rises, we all rise.

Daryl Chang

1. You are conscious always and know who you are: God.

    That is, you know nothing of Satan and its concepts.

    You know only of perfection and perfect good.

2. You make love and its derivatives (ie. joy, peace, happiness, et cetera) the solitary habit in all your thoughts, words, feelings, and actions.

    The mind of God is pure and loving.

    You have unwavering beautiful, loving, courageous, and pure thoughts of yourself and of the world every moment.

    That is, you never allow fear and its derivatives (ie. anger, hatred, greed, envy, anxiety, et cetera) into your being.

    Love and fear are like light and darkness.

    When complete light enters, all darkness disappears.

    You are able to properly fulfill your desires when love wholly enters and you completely let go of fear.

3. You truly see and know only Oneness: God.

    That is, you never see and know duality or separation of any kind.

    Nothing is separate from you.

    You never judge, criticize, or condemn anyone or anything.

4. You know you are the creator of everything you experience in your world.

    That is, you know all are of your own doing.

    You know that you are the one in control and no one else external to you is responsible for your experiences.

There is not someone somewhere who has control over you or controlling your circumstances.

Everything is a reflection or projection of you and undesirable experiences mean you still have hidden issues of duality and have not reconciled the true nature of Oneness.

There are no random people, places, and events.

Nothing is separate from you.

With the realization that you create everyone and everything (ie. the "bad" persons are acting out the roles you have given them and the learning experiences you have scripted), you recognize that everyone and everything is actually innocent.

With this realization, you are conscious of Oneness – they are all you; we are all one.

With this realization, you forgive everyone and everything.

With this realization, you embrace love toward all.

5. You accept full responsibility for yourself, your actions, and your life.

   That is, you do not abdicate your personal responsibility to choose correct over incorrect action to someone else.

   You actions and responsibilities are always your own.

   You stop blaming another or others for your state of affairs.

   You are your own authority.

6. You give your undivided attention and thoughts to God and his kingdom only.

   Wherever you give your attention, you give your power.

   You do not give to what you do not want to expand.

That is, you never give your attention and thoughts to any aspect or concept of Satan (ie. conspiracies, aliens, war, vengeance, tyrants, murderers, poverty, dis-ease, death, evil, et cetera) so as to not create, grow, or sustain it further.

7.   You know all is spiritual.

That is, you know that the intimate thoughts you have in spirit are the originating causes of the physical world you express and experience.

When you have undesirable physical circumstances, you do not try to manipulate them but instead look to what they are there to teach you about yourself and to change the thoughts that are creating them.

When you have undesirable physical circumstances, you recognize you have unresolved issues of duality that you still need to reconcile.

8.   You express constant gratitude toward God and all your circumstances.

That is, you show continuous love in every present moment of the now, shifting your focus from what you consider a bad, negative, or undesired experience to gratitude for the divine learning experience it provides you to grow and achieve your highest self.

You realize, accept, and know you are given everything and are provided for always hence you are in constant gratitude.

9.   You give everything of yourself freely to maintain the flow of God through yourself and all.

You know giving and receiving are one of the same.

What you give to others, you give to yourself; what you give to yourself, you give to others.

When you love yourself, you love God; when you love God, you love yourself.

When you help others, you help yourself; when you help yourself, you help others.

This is God flow.

10. You know you are eternal and infinite.

    You no longer fear death but love life.

    You focus your attention on the pure joy of being and the self-expression of your unique perspective and talents to blossom an aspect of natural intelligence that has never been expressed before.

www.ingramcontent.com/pod-product-compliance
Lightning Source LLC
Chambersburg PA
CBHW060054050426
42448CB00011B/2448